DECENCY

by Lauren Crowley

Copyright © 2017 by Lauren Crowley

All rights reserved. No part of this book may be used or reproduced in any manner whatsoever without written permission except in the case of brief quotations embodied in critical articles and reviews.

First paperback edition published in 2017 by Crowley Press
CrowleyPress.com

Printed in the United States of America

Library of Congress Cataloging-in-Publication Data
ISBN-13: 978-0-9982322-2-5
ISBN-10: 099823222X
1. Poetry 2. Women authors

Also by Lauren Crowley:

BAPTISM

BLOOD BODY

Decency

DECENCY

He carried me down the stairs to a dungeon I had dreamt of.
I wept at the sight, there were no walls, no walls, no walls.

I sat alone.

January 15, 2017

CROWLEY

Decency, cut me clean.
I feel your old scratches,
though they are very weak.

And I remember your hands,
meager and shy. I cut you with
roses, you claw at my eyes.

Meager and shy,
meager and shy.

My hands have grown heavy;
in the dark they are blind.

January 16, 2017

DECENCY

Woman with two bibles cursed me under her breath

My hands fell apart and I was afraid,

woman with two bibles cursed me,

reciting the end times, demons like to talk about

the end times

January 20, 2017

CROWLEY

Sometimes I stare into flames and they speak to me, and I wonder, is there anything to know that isn't already inside of me. Have I ever told a true story, and do I have anything left to tell. I keep pointing at a box of things gone by when they ask who I am. I think the boxes are really empty, I haven't taken a peek. I miss thinking my boxes were full. Now I'm only an arrow, pointing at things far away. And these things I can't speak.

I'm taking a journey not many understand. What unseen force controls me, the wind? the water? the moon? Some are happy to be possessed. A will is a will, they say.

I kiss myself, I am a faithful lover. I follow through. How else could I have found someone like me? Consistency, every morning the sun asks me: are you ready? And I say yes, the plans have not changed. The voice is still strong, breathing in my ear.

I am these visions. I'm pulled towards them, like the tides. I think they're the reason I'm alive.

January 20, 2017

DECENCY

What part of me is holy,
what could the nuns nod at,
what rests on the altar, next to
the tabernacle. Where is my
tabernacle? Where am I locked?
Where is my blessed body?

Saved, what is salvation,
which god accepts me,
and which part of me
does he accept...

What part of me is holy,
what part of me is holy,
what part of me is

We were never naked,
my bed was velvet,
and my heart was
what it was

I chose a serpent,
not a god

(I am a serpent,
not a god)

January 22, 2017

CROWLEY

I am tired,
death is tiring.
Look at my face,
pinkening like a peach,
marie antoinette, before
the crown, rococo, gilded
frown.

Birth is tiring,
raising the baby is
tiring, motherhood,
tiring, I am a nothing
whose dreams are too
big, cut open the belly
to let it all in.

I am tired,
but I hold the child
in my arms, and tonight
it is small. We rest. I sleep.
My hair grows long and it
grows tall.

January 23, 2017

DECENCY

My sheets smell like caramel 'cause I slept in them too long
Crabs prefer shells, crabapples, the floor, where they ripen and die

I prefer lying on top of you, below you, by you, sigh

Cream-filled croissant, I am a raindrop.

The witch's frog, and every smiling log,

floating down our river, joy.

January 24, 2017

CROWLEY

Lust takes a breath but
stands behind walls,
invisible skin,
what illusions will fall,

and what is presence,
We only know truth.

Something told by the body,
but not of it-

I love it,
let it fall

January 26, 2017

DECENCY

A gasp, offensive, what do we take seriously, I'm friends with Sade,
I'm laughing.

And, yet,

I was once a girl, too.

Vulgarize me, vulgarize me,
there is no skin left, there is

the crying earth-shattering shame,
we will play its games.

Blinded, raped, lame-

Decapitate me, then I will
breathe.

January 27, 2017

Flagellation, torture, worship, horror,

am I hurting myself? am I hurting
myself? am I hurting myself,
am I hurting,

January 27, 2017

DECENCY

There are chapels and there are hells,
I awoke with no religion,
like a leaf, like a pot,
like a being with no thought,

Philosophic, I am not,

Barbarism, Dionysus,

an undone knot.

We are dancers, the night is humid,

her mind is a web, I AM NOT CAUGHT!

January 28, 2017

CROWLEY

Drowned again.

Primordial chaos, confusion,

the whole of the sea is inside me.

So is something else,

and it will save me.

January 28, 2017

DECENCY

All it takes is a few good screams,

lightness, you follow me about,

saying: 'listen' and I do,

but I don't, and I promise,

I will hold you, like the

bird that you are, lightness,

you follow me everyday.

From now on I will follow

you.

January 28, 2017

Am I a poet or am I sucking at my own wound, the snake bite, I can taste the poison but I can't remember being bit

January 30, 2017

DECENCY

Cherry bowl, lover,
girl, eat them one by one
and at the bottom of blue
porcelain, an old key, as
resonant as a blurring
body, the one key, the
one key, the one key,
the soul speaks, will
I listen? Trust

and faith.

We made a choice, today.

Trust, trust
and faith.

January 30, 2017

CROWLEY

the door to the occult is shaped like a woman

it's shaped like me

just like me, sigh,

we've been here before,

devil locked in her case,

coffin, seductrix, satan

occult leader in the making

follow me but I'll lead you
to a dark room and then
leave you,

I am an anima and an animus,
too.

January 31, 2017

DECENCY

butterfly waits in her lair
to scream

to Scream, I say,
mean mean mean

we carry these things,
oh how we carry these things!

the heart's a queen,
I am full of these things

Restless and wander and
simmering heat

I'm full of these things

I don't want to deceive

It's not good for my back
It's not good for my feet,

I keep my mouth closed
to hide my sharp teeth

(truly, I'm weak
I'll break or I'll bleed)

February 2, 2017

CROWLEY

there's a lake in the backyard and
I dream of serpents rising out of it,
dolphins, swimming, I dreamt of
the tallest figure, a silhouette in black,
rising up, that I could not watch

that I could not watch

black things rise out of me,
too, I scream in the car but
still there is that thing, centuries old,
the snarl, every resistance, every king

which layer of hell do I preside over
and what do I say when I crack
in half,

the dark army charges forward,
as the lining of my skin lays on
the floor

February 3, 2017

DECENCY

there is nothing underneath this skin, I say, just
pretty blush pink, I'm just a soft fleshy thing,
the moon and its tides don't recognize me,
I'm just a pearly dripping thing, no moods
inside of me,

February 6, 2017

CROWLEY

Virgo

Indominance,
In my sepulcher,
Submission is safe.

We can take turns on our knees,
but I'll stay there longer.

I'll be your locked room,
promised to you

Fortress, foreseeable future,
Pillage me,

Robber

(white knees, white knees, bite into me,
an unripe fruit)

February 7, 2017

DECENCY

a moan or
a wish or
a scream,

inoperable things

February 7, 2017

The heart is too big, the surgeons say. But if we take it out or chop off a bit, it will all fall apart. Or it will all be meaningless. It all rests on this heart, we do not understand it, but every veins leads to it, and every breath feeds it, and if she tries to get it out of her mind, she goes mad. The heart was the compass all along, and to not take its orders was to fall into anomie, disarray, chaos. Chaos, she thought, the waves are chaos. She said, chop my body in two. Drain out the blood. Maybe I'll feel less. Maybe pain will become a myth. Maybe I won't be me.

Maybe she was missing the point.

The surgeons sewed her up. They pinned a note to her chest, a short letter, apologizing for the confusion, most aren't born with to-do lists, or explanations.

"If you don't listen to it it will all fall apart. This you know, this I know, these aren't tales that you can choose to ignore. These aren't whims or ghosts or frauds. These are the whisperings of a too big heart."

She awoke with an excuse, with permission. An explanation, doctor's orders!

Listen to your too big heart,
listen to your too big heart,
listen to your too big,

and then it became small. The giant sleeps, it shrinks, it awakens, it catches flame, it thinks, it reads, it falls into place. The heart is too big, they say.

Don't wish it away, you're a fool, let it stay.

February 8, 2017

DECENCY

I could open my mouth wider,
I could stick out my tongue,
perhaps catch one lick of
water, feed me, I'm numb

I want to return to myself -
what keeps me away, what
shackles me, I'm fallen,
I'm hardening, I'm
worn.

freedom as a memory

freedom as a hope

(A divine laugh, we are bound to one path,
and we will do what we must, to return to it.)

February 9, 2017

CROWLEY

princess,

girl with soft feet,
soft hands,

pearls and pomme frites,

awaiting a mermaid to
suffocate me,

kidnap my heart
there's nothing here to be seen,

pearls and pomme frites,

you terrorize me

descend into me,
I don't want to be seen
I must hide in this dream
until there's nothing left but
me,

a rose that will drip
until I cut myself clean

February 10, 2017

DECENCY

As soon as I named the animal, I was calm. It was running about and someone pointed to it and said 'that is yours' and I had to agree. It will sit with me and I with it. It's so tired from running, I'm so torn from denying, splitting, I used to pick at my split ends, hiding the duality, I used to go mad, eyes went black, madness, madness, mad woman, miles from there, and yet- I feel the old icy burn. Hand at my throat, red lights, silent siren, on my knees now, trying to get away, too big to hide, too wide to deny. Soft skies, there are soft skies, nightmares rise, let me do a breathing exercise, except that doesn't work, does it. Let me be with him, let me stay, let me tame this animal today. It is mine. I am quick to deny, but I'll keep it. Perhaps it will die of old age, whither away. I've had it since I was nine, I'd say, no tears at its passing. And then, oh and then, like a madwoman, I'd run. No haunting, no guns. A girl unprotected.

February 11, 2017

I wanted to become a death doula. I said, I know how to die, I've done it before. Mothers having babies were practicing an art I was not skilled at, because every birth was tenuous, tentative, and my hands shook too much to be tender. Death, too, had a question mark. The rubble has its ghosts. A hand reaching out from a grave, to clasp at our ankles. Yes, immortality belongs to the things we want dead.

And I can't help hovering over the crib, listening for the baby's breath. I don't want it to suffocate, I say, as I stand far too close.

February 11, 2017

DECENCY

An ocean at my disposal. That's why I write.
But I'd rather be the pen, I'd rather be the fire,
than every tidal wave I've known. I'd rather be
the woman whose writing is shaped like the sea,
I'd rather be, I'd rather be.

There's a sunken ship, but I'm not on it.

There's the woman who dreamt of drowning,
but never did. That's me, that's me.

February 11, 2017

CROWLEY

To tell a true story,

I was born and tied into a knot. I was good at art. I was good at keeping secrets, at being a secret. I began to divulge at twenty-one, but by twenty-three, I had to confess: I wanted to be private. I turned away like the dark face of the moon.

Can't you just read this?

I was born a red knot. And I grew an eleventh finger to pry it loose. At night I was a red sea, I slept more than others, I was pulled to my own spreading out.

While one hand loosens, the other has an urge to pull tight - perhaps we can rip it in two. A tension rises and now there is the scream.

Collapse- there is no collapse. I'm still a knot.

But I still pick it apart at night with my nails. One night you'll arrive and I'll be undone.

There is a future in my mind, where I've come undone. And it smells like cinnamon, like gold glow and cinnamon, the brown deepens until we are like soil.

February 12, 2017

DECENCY

Nothing will grab my attention like a spider eating its prey. Its power to devour- I'm sure it feels no guilt.

February 12, 2017

I can be beautiful, I say, as I fall to the floor. Mothers can be beautiful, motherhood, beautiful. Mary, beautiful. I am like Mary. I am in blue, and I am unscathed, and I hold this sorrow, and I fall away.

Mother Mary hold me
Mother Mary hold me
Mother Mary hold me
I am gone

February 13, 2017

DECENCY

The storm! the sea,
don't terrorize me,
I don't want to be free,
for I'll fall on my feet,
but see, but see,
don't you listen to me
I don't know what I need
I think, I think,
a whirlwind spiral
to keep me from
feeling

Oh those women with their emotions and their hearts on their sleeve,

I want to be real,

a girl with sharp teeth.

February 13, 2017

Lawless

Some are born lawless (they know they are lawless and so they are lawless)

I was born lawless, and when I hear of the others, it's like hearing an old tune,

golden, and loving. golden, and true

February 13, 2017

DECENCY

it seems that all along I was in a forest of my own,
the nightmare was, that every match might be lit
and thrown into it, so easily.

there is a wide sanctuary inside, and I know it,
(now), and I see that two ships sailing next to
one another for an indeterminate time, that
is forever, in a way of its own. isn't it. aren't
I fortunate, for knowing you at all.

my tree stands tall, now that I
remember it.

February 16, 2017

CROWLEY

I came from a star that burns just a bit brighter,
hotter, heat is my resurrection, heat is my truth,
what is it, anxiety at our condition, who looks
into my eyes and sees a dungeon inside, the
way I spring up, again and again, positively
entranced, a certain distance, a wall much
too wide, to hide the satyrs' dance.

Some of us are born engorged, unripened fruit,
behind a wall, one peephole to show us the
secret of it all,

Would you say I'm lying?

Some truths are undisturbed,
slumbering awake, or never heard

Some truths rule them all.

I am a lightening rod of desire,
or I'm nothing at all.

(Furor, desire, furor, desire, furor, desire...)

February 16, 2017

DECENCY

"All I want to be is an artist" she said, with her feet on the floor. All I want to be is a collector of thoughts, tied in a bow, one who sees butterfly wings peeking out from burnt leaves. All I want to be is a mother, your own waterfall. "All I want to be is an artist" I said, with my hand out for more.

Heart-strings, nothing but these, don't I have something to give, too?

I'll give you me

February 16, 2017

I pressed my cheek to the wood and my lips to the grate,
"I think what I can't quite admit is that I'd risk getting hurt, that if there is a cliff, I will dive, others live inland, you see. You know this, I do, too. Can we call it surrender? Will you call it that, with me? I am like the saints. There is something in me that is like them. Do you believe me when I say that? I don't mind being blasphemous, I'm just here to figure this out. I'm the truest thing you'll ever see, these words, they're just glimpses, the truth is a black black hole and we'd all be destroyed. Or restored, restored by it. That's always how it is, isn't it. What if I tell you I'm a fallen woman. You'd believe me then. I fall so easily, my heart has its weight. But it also has wings!

"Like an angel. Do you see what I mean? There is beauty in all things. Christ's beauty, I'll let you call it that. We're all his children, aren't we. I'm a child no more. Haven't been one for awhile. But I'm something else now, like the doll you've left in the closet. Old but new. There's more I could tell you. Could I tell you a lie? No, we know I don't do that. My eyes will always speak. Could you speak for me? Could someone please tell him? That I'd lie on a bed of nails, that I'd let them pierce my throat, oh, I'm getting carried away. Who is it that carries my body away from the place where I collapse. And do I ever really collapse, I sleep with one eye open, the other two closed. You know what I mean by that, and you know I'm dressed in purple. And you know that blasphemy is my throne, and the mind looks like a dagger, you know there's more to romance than they tell you.

"And we'd die for it. Wouldn't we. We are knights, we are virgins. We are every battle in which love was won."

February 16, 2017

DECENCY

lamiae,

whose feet are unformed and
whose waists bend and wave,
beautiful beings. I have seen
your long face, and the way
that it craves, an inch from
depraved, it just takes and
it takes, I am an

open mouth. dying for one
taste.

I am a mother
whose fingers
dip into the grave

February 18, 2017

I am single-minded,
a maid to my own
blooming. I feed on
visions, I make promises,
I sleep like an angel, whose
hands are for making, it comes
from the ether or it comes from
the clay, like a dream of a god I
make my own image, myself,
oh visions, you are the fabric
I wear. You are my long brown
hair. I'm longing to rehearse you,
you're a daimon, I'm ensnared.

February 18, 2017

DECENCY

Dear Lord,

You have seen me through clouds, the fog of the morning. Am I an echo to you? Do you see me circling, around my own wishing fountain, skirting the center, my one true home. You know not the voice that shouts from the corner, or states plainly, putting things into perspective. Pragmatism. A side-effect of living. An enemy worth beseeching. Dear Lord, I've forgotten my wings. Now if you could meet me on every corner with a handwritten note, I'd start believing.

You know I already do, more than most, I'm a faith-ridden follower, a fool, or a wanderer. If I write you letters it's only to let you know I'm still alive. I was a seeker who wandered home, and slept for twenty-five days, and now I'm awake, but I need your encouragement. You made the artists, too.

And I am like the moon, if the moon was on fire, a woman whose shadow rises like smoke. And so forgive me if I find a goddess wiser, and forgive me if I am my own god. I think you made me this way. I think for it I am better.

Sincerely,
Sincerity's daughter

February 18, 2017

I want to be free, I let the night engulf me, the storm warms my cheek, I was born by the sea, or I died by the sea, on a cliff as a woman who no longer was free.

I know I'm made for something more. I know I can't wait for what is in store. I know I will fall to my knees on the floor, I know I want more. I know there is more.

February 20, 2017

DECENCY

Eroticism, a long snake. In a cave I pass by every day.

I'm thinking about going in.

I'm thinking of moving into my veins.

We'll get used to the red of the sky and the way

that every last cell is marked with my name,

we'll get used to our nature, its bleeding, our pain.

I think I'll fall asleep in this cave.

In a dream oh so red I will sin and I'll sway.

February 21, 2017

Peak moments, pure, our essence, true nature, that which we seek at the bottom of things, and that which we dance with in the midst of our dreams,

The body has its own, and the spirit follows through, I'm trying to love everything that I do, because

conditions become four walls and a room, a place where I'm chained by my own disapproval,

I'd rather be dead, than to live out a lie. I'm fighting my way to the other side,

the top of a hill. A sustained, peak moment. A world with no rooms.

I thought I could be myself. First, I must choose.

February 21, 2017

DECENCY

Behind door number nine is every ocean that swept me up and I loved to drown, for once I was water and I became so light that I knew to carry me didn't mean much, no burden, no harm, just lift me by the arms, I'm a saint, I'm a sinner, whichever you prefer, I'll be good I'll be bad I will flatten myself out and be the floor beneath your feet, I'm an open mouth and not much else. Encased in black latex or the shadow of this room, I'll disappear for you. I'll be a ghost! Or a phantom or your shadow or a fantasy or your mother. I'll be your daughter, I'll be unclean. I'll be the ocean and let you drown, too.

February 22, 2017

CROWLEY

I unfurled like a smoke curl under the veil of their eyes, I was every monster that could be craved, I transformed into a demi-god as I sat in their gaze. I am an

open wound, whose opening entrances and invites, in the depths of my being there is something divine. And I know it, and I want it, and I'm with it all the time.

The door to that something is opening tonight, I fell to my knees, and worshipped my own mind.

February 22, 2017

DECENCY

I floated in with hesitation, because I remembered the times before.
But the promise of love, and life, filled my bones, my weeping cosmic bones. I came in with one vision, one thing in mind.

But birth and life are like tidal waves sinking us down, the salt in our mouth distracts, our eyes close and we forget.

I came down with one vision, and with your eyes in mind.

I knew I would find you, somewhere in time.

February 26, 2017

Not all mothers cry, some are the basins of rivers and they have been for years, a pillar of earth, made moist by the tears of their youth, their womb is the red that endures, the core, oh whore, how many children do you keep, even the cats that sleep at your feet, even the men who cling to you in sleep, even the river.

February 27, 2017

DECENCY

Rose feet-
the water became sweet
as my eyes lit up
with the promise
of there

And I'm feeling and dreaming
and my naked heart's clinging
to the promise
of there,

its tendrils, my hair,
its soft breathing stare

I've been locked in its lair
In the light of the morning
I know I am there

March 1, 2017

I can't spare a drop, I said,

not in this drought.

Are we fools for believing in an endless rain?

Am I a fool for believing in fate?

March 3, 2017

DECENCY

Unhappy mornings,
I'm an honest person,
who can only crumble
for so long. We can talk
about phoenixes and flames
but sometimes I tire of dying,
I thought I had grasped at life
but I chose to be boring, thinking
there's an ounce of happiness in
giving in. But I can't hide these
wings I can't hide these teeth
for much longer.

I'm ancient but learning,
and I may be masochistic,
but not for such ugly chains.

March 4, 2017

If I am a star who yearns to collapse in on itself, if only to create more light, blink twice. If some part of me is angelic, and if I have the power to heal, leave a feather in my wake. If two hands will catch me when I finally choose to jump, sing me something familiar as I fall asleep. I am looking for signs, pretending to be blind. A priest has doubts, even when the flames of faith burn bright.

If I am a creator, like they say I am, let me create.

March 5, 2017

DECENCY

To become lunar you must stop lying (to yourself) and start lying (to others) the way the moon lies behind clouds on the days we want to see it. To become lunar you must dip yourself in glass, until you are nothing but smooth. You let your eyes get glassy, soft, wet. You stay attracted to the violent women until you see you are just like them, and then the fusion of self and other becomes a form of self love that sustains and heals. You become childlike without apologizing. And you set your womanhood on a table by the window and watch it grow, it breathes like a plant underwater, it seethes. And if you are very lucky its vines will curl around each limb of yours until you are strangled by it, entangled by it, and then you will know ecstasy, and then you will fall to the floor, and have only one tear to spare, the excess of acceptance. The church and its reverence.

To become lunar you must decide to be lunar.

March 5, 2017

Were some of us born to be two eyes beholding the golden hour before dusk? Throats for holding and for singing, were some of us born for just this? As poets and as lovers, as women who flit and lay, as singers. As the lighters of incense, as angels that breathe upon the earth. As something else. Not for somewhere else, but maybe as reminders of somewhere else.

March 6, 2017

DECENCY

The carved heart, like a gutted deer, whose eyes seem to follow you, when it's mounted on the wall. I named him *jalousie* but I could have named him *holeness*, for he is hollow. I think at night he eats my flesh, and because he has always been there I don't know how to make it stop. Because his eyes have always locked with mine and transmitted to me some sort of panic, because he is mounted on the wall, I must become hollow too, on the worst nights. When it comes to throwing him out, I am unsure, because could he not raise up, as the dead do, and come back into my house? He becomes a ghost when I look into your eyes. Only then. Your brown is warmer than his death.

March 7, 2017

CROWLEY

Can you tell that there are so few words left, it is like death but with no sense of renewal, no wind behind me, whispering 'feel your death, and feel the layers beneath become born.' No. There is none of that, just a steady pounding into the floor, but I am not flat, I become an uncomfortable curl, a deadened pile. They're keeping me just alive, just alive, so that I may not die and rise away. Do you see the lack of words, of something to say? I am not empty, my insides have become thick, heavy, far too solid. Almost dry earth. Vegetable woman. Stale cake.

I can't even dream of a moist ravine where I run away, hide behind rocks and the trees where I'm safe. Safe... I've been abandoned to a family that's neither fatal or safe. And so I'm pulling apart and yet I must be sewn up for the day, what makes me normal will eventually lacerate. Like a bracelet too tight. Like I'm testing my fate.

Like I need to be rescued - but I'm the knight and the maid.

March 7, 2017

DECENCY

Could we just admit to being a woman, oh, but no, some part of us is sharp, the mind, rarely languid, always these nerves, electric and unbearing, am I fecund or am I singular, a being who only creates himself, what children do I cradle, when for so many hours I am alone. Alone amongst others, for I am the outsider, looking in. Looking in and not liking what I see, oh I don't mean to be so full of superiority. Even as a woman, I will live in the clouds. I will scale each ivory tower like a very large spider, but I won't stay for long. Because I have memories of the floor, of a hole in the wall. Where I become languid, where I become more. A spreading apart, no legs no arms no utility, no work. We work at this, at languidity. At animalism. At a sainthood of the water, it makes the earth more.

I am holy for trying, for drifting further from this shore.

(I will sink into myself and then turn around. I will meet the abyss and through it, be restored.)

March 7, 2017

CROWLEY

The past doesn't exist they say so I pretend that it doesn't, and it becomes this bruised color thing in the sky, radiation, a purpling shadow above me, always a reminder of what was and what wasn't. I want to cut it out of me.

I regret every time I speak of it, and I only do it to mirror you.

You speak of it like it doesn't float in the sky.

You speak of it like it doesn't gnaw at my side.

I will become an atheist to it, no hells, no far away heaven, no ghosts, no ghosts, NO GHOSTS! And no gods, other than this love.

March 7, 2017

DECENCY

There is a garden inside of my chest, I can feel it, like some promise, something foretold. I could feel it the other day, as I clung to your waist, it has been the orange line through all of our days. I am orange with you, I am orange for you, you are orange with me, I am orange for you. The garden grows everyday. And its gates open wider.

March 7, 2017

CROWLEY

I say 'I Surrender' and wave my white flag
but I painted it over, it used to be red

Will I fight 'til I'm dead? But death doesn't come.
I won't bow my head when I know of the Sun.

Depravity I can do, but any slavery's a noose-
and really what is there to surrender to?

March 8, 2017

DECENCY

What will I call beautiful next - where will I cast the plutonian seed, saying, there is a dark art in every body of imagination, in every seduction, in every gagging cry. If only I could be a bit more free... and this is where I find art, this is the door through which I move, saying, let us leave morality behind, let us leave our preconceptions, and our clothes, and our names. This is when I kiss your fingers like a starlit night, and I laugh until dawn. This is where I need you, this is where I need myself. This is the hole of vanquishing, where every scar melts off.

And I lie on the floor like a madwoman, like when ecstasy coursed through my veins, and I said "I love you I love you I love you" and I became pink.

I am a yellow heart for you, the center of each flame.

I am named and unnamed.

March 8, 2017

CROWLEY

Because I wander, I require chains.

Bites and a brick to the head, I will make a list of things that make me feel here. Oh I'm annoyed that I'm not quite of the body, that I am a sensual beast who lives in dreams. Oh the world of phantasy is like a color we have not seen, and the syrup of the heart is like hard alcohol to me, oh the body beats briefly, and lightly, I never could find my own pulse.

Will life ever be like a dream? like a fantasy? not ideal, no, but visceral, clutching, unfettered. Oh, how I live in the drama of power and domination, I'm just looking for a weight to hold me down. I flit off.... and I am disturbed, by the thoughts that fly around my head like flies, oh they are stronger than my dreams when I'm awake. No therapy quiets them down. I only need sleep, I only want sleep, and to escape away, through the portal at the back of my mind.

Presence isn't anything. The world and its makings only reach me through the ear of my mind. I am far - but when I get close, like a fish against the tide, I feel farther than that. I will go the other way. And drift off 'til I'm real real real. Real something, real something, real I swear. I'm not real I swear.

(is that okay? why? how not to be-)

Dream girl only exists in her dream world, really.

I feel sick, what does it even mean.

I am Jesus's tear, it fell to earth when we told his story, and I am also the paintbrush, and even sex. But I don't understand it.

Maybe if I bleed, maybe if I'm born... please, pierce me with any spear, any will do, something through me until the end of time.

(Called: how do I explain that I'm not here. And how do I stop it.)

Let my soul be involved, boy, oh, oh, oh, oh, oh... Sweetness. All that joy-

March 9, 2017

DECENCY

You see if you grab into my stomach, if you tear deep into that flesh, and tear at it, go into me, grab from the inside, if you make me open, I will feel better.

A gaping wound - what better doorway is there, oh I just need to bleed a little just let me bleed a little, oh I just need to bleed a little, won't you let me bleed a little, oh oh oh, oh. Oh.

Stab into the shadow of me-

March 9, 2017

CROWLEY

I can't lie about what shade of red I am, any longer... and no I have not lied, but I've pretended, and I've feigned, and I've hidden it, I still will hide it, like something sacred, not for all eyes whose gaze will dry it, I am the same color of red as the first explosion. Or at least that is what I will say. (I am much richer than that...)

There is only the red and we know it, we know it well. Let us stop pretending.

March 10, 2017

DECENCY

Let me be at peace with the desire I bring, let me be at peace. The woman in me sleeps. No one told her that her dream's complete.

March 13, 2017

I'm full of fluidity, if only, if only, oh maybe, oh maybe,

And yet I was a dream every time, a dream in green,

every moment the dream, the soul paints this, as I

sit back and wonder what more could I do, like a

path could never be below my feet, like there's a

path at all. Or maybe there's just each day and

how well I play me.

And perhaps every point to me is Paris and

every arm divine, oh but yours, oh but yours,

is the one without time. I'll call you mine-

March 13, 2017

DECENCY

While she sleeps we cover the floor in furs. We light every candle, write her a note, oh love, you must rest, the moon shines upon you, and you are at one. And then we sell all the bronze for a promise of gold, we know that something will take and then it will grow, and I will leave my own notes on the piers and the floors, on every park bench and decide to be more, oh more, oh more, oh the king of the moors, I feed on a fog and free myself with this sword, am I a duke or a poet, am I a black tall horse? I've surrendered to this maybe, I think I'm back on course.

March 13, 2017

Where was she when she was twenty-four? they'll ask and then they'll read this, and they'll know that she sat with the windows open in a blue dress, as a record was playing, and she thought about what she had to say, and how others had messages but she only had soft fabrics, gleaming jewels, and some love. At twenty-four she was a believer with her hands out, will it rain? she asks, she won't believe it until her hands are wet. She believes enough to cup her hands, though.

Is there someone, many someones, that could perhaps cup their hands, too, and let me be the rain for them? Do you like soft fabrics, too?

Do you like what I write, do you like me?

March 14, 2017

DECENCY

To write well is just a petal, on a flower whose center is more than god's gift, oh to feel, to feel! And to feel well, to be the woman standing on a cliff above the ocean, the water may lick her cheeks but always she stands apart from its waves and its wails. The woman who can throw every old locket and every disappointment into this sea, they were never really hers. I'm tired of empowerment, whatever happened to the curl of a seashell, a woman falling asleep. What happened to the women like me?

No I did not climb a mountain to give you a sermon, no I'm not really concerned with being an inspiration, unless you're a woman like me, and you have your own oceans, well maybe you'll touch them like they're not really poisonous, and maybe you'll live like you're meant to, yes the both of us, and maybe I'll go down in history, notorious, and maybe I'll become a Christian, glorious, the light it doesn't end, and femininity is known to bend, so let us bend like water, let us burn our own funeral pyres, let us be women. A prayer-

March 14, 2017

A woman has two tongues and she has a snake writhing through her belly, I am writing from a convent in the dark of a city, I was blessed by our Lord for being free of vanity, but he doesn't know me, but he doesn't know. And he called me immaculate but I've been touched by everything, His fingers were cold. And I had a sour feeling that he was so small, and there was a backdrop behind him, the source and the All. The place where I came from, the place I call Home. It knows me much more. I am heaven's whore, and when I wear white they call me Mater, and because I am me I will fall to the floor, I will writhe and I'll moan, I'm Semper Virgo.

March 15, 2017

DECENCY

I think if I wasn't shy I would be a singer,
and maybe if I didn't wear that cage I would let you hear it, too,
and I wouldn't seize up when I try to talk to you,
there is a deep water, where I often wade,
and I thought I could go this whole time without
giving you a taste of it, oh,

I didn't mean to hide away. I didn't mean to I didn't mean to

(In my heart) I imagine a creaking door, open just an inch,
I didn't say a word, but I opened it, and it's never been open,
not really, no, and I've never really been known, oh, don't you
see, the oblivion I've lived in, the way I've gone on alone-

Don't you see, you've only stood by my windows

(There is a large large house and inside there is terror.
And inside of that there is hope.)

March 15, 2017

CROWLEY

Can I love all the water in me? all that water? all that sea?

I wouldn't rain on you if it were up to me...

And yet you seem to breathe underwater,

like you're my symbiotic partner,

and maybe being water won't
be the death of me.

March 16, 2017

DECENCY

Moon:

I remember a time when I was like you - when I was rounded, and glowing, and feminine, too. When I sat up above like a queen of the night, and I was so sure. I let the sureness wash over me like a warm-hooded body and it made it all right. It was always all right. I was once like you and I stood tall, and I was brave, and my doubt was small, do you remember me this way? You watched over me then, too. I slept under your skin and dreamt of shadows of blue. You remember me well. You called out my name - the one that only we know, the one released from shame. You remember my star. You remember my rings. You remember everything- in front of you I sing.

I think I'll stop creating for awhile, I think I'll just write. Like a songbird moving upwards, awakening from the night... I need another exorcism. And I need it by tonight.

I seemed chained to a delusion, a ball of fear, a ruining. I'm not really like this, am I? Because when there's a seed to suffer, I seem to be full of water, and every bag of fertilizer is poured upon its wake. And yet eternal love seems to rise above its fall, like an alternate realty that waits for me to break.

I'll break. And surrender to your oceans, that is the magic potion, surrender to our fates.

Moon, I am just like you. A myth of grand proportions. And tonight there's just one battle, emotion and the brain.

March 17, 2017

Can we love ourselves under the star of Cathexis?
Can I gather up each piece of me that I give to you and
clone it, one for me and one for you, so I can become
something other than an empty basket, what a racket,
to love is to divest. Or so I thought, or so I did, until I
became completely transparent, a ghost, an echo, oh,
to love is to give yourself up. And how some of us want that,
the mind-obliterators, the meditators, the sleepers. The shadows...

I'm waiting to be an empty plane so we can start all over.
Give me seven days and I'll create just what I want,
a softer voice, a stronger heart.

A sense of being solid,
a self that does not depart.

March 18, 2017

DECENCY

Blessed, heaven, arms around me, tightly,
every inner voice leads me to a gold gleaming meadow,
oh, how I'd like to give in, and wake up an angel, who says
every morning: my wings are real. And to feel, and to let it
pass away, and to gather up my strength, and to be a beginning.
Every evening is for soul, every eleven o'clock, every noon. Every
four, if there is a mission to know then I must know it, and if there's
a raison d'être, I must be it, and if there's me and you, I must believe
it, and I just want to say that we already know it, and feel it, and find
ourselves waking up in the dream like we planned it, and there are
centuries leading up to this point, I saw a life long ago, and my soul
said 'this was my favorite', and well what's this one to me? Perhaps
it's the brightest. A star burns in a collision, a heart mends in a sky
above the ocean, and I find a groove to hold me, just hold me, every
eleven o'clock, every noon, every two. I'll sell my soul to you, it rises
up amongst our waves, it kisses, it crashes, it remembers fate.

I remember you.

March 19, 2017

CROWLEY

Aries,
Return to me the bottled up flame, oh, which bed did I leave it under,
and which spirit will return it to me. Oh my soul is bursting with a taste for
unity, like I spread little bits of myself across a planet long ago, I will
travel through time to get them. Oh,

where is desire, and who am I, clawed feet, or kneeling girl,

I will scrape my way to the essence of me,

I will love this light, new morning,

I will explode again.

Adulthood and sin, the sacred garden,
who am I, a riddle, what's important,
what am I trying to say...

Every morning I will set my self aflame.

Sea creature who learned how to burn.

scream it out, sing it, desire is quiet, the body's a moan

March 20, 2017

DECENCY

My heart is a tired little thing,
and I am as soft as a pastry cream,
and am spoiled just as easily, my
heart is a bent bird with shivering
wings, I am foolish foolish foolish
for allegiance to a dream,

I want to be pure -
I want to know of surrender,

to the things that fill up me,
unlight, unwings

I am moving forward,
I'm moving in

March 22, 2017

Crucified woman

a smile on the cross,
we are light light light,
light as an inchworm clinging to its wood,
I found you in my soul, as I find this, and so
lift me up, I want to be taken, and when I awaken,
each morning is for truth, oh, don't you see how I
sleep, upon my own cross, don't you see that I'm
nailed, or tied, or broken, because life will stomp
every last lie out of you. Life won't leave you alone.

And so it is. And so it's bliss, and so when I go to
here from there, I am holy, Mary was a god, too,
and we rest easy. I am an image of flesh, pinned
down to my own divinity. Oh Goddess Goddess
godness, even my bones sing for it-

March 23, 2017

DECENCY

I imagined a nosebleed,

(as I walked into work,
what gush in me will
feign to deceive a
composure so constructed
by a twig and a leaf,)

we pray for a leak;
could I be exposed
as a woman or freak?

March 23, 2017

CROWLEY

I want it to rain.

A part of me pours,
and I am the leak,
the tear, the hole,

the blue-wed night,
and that star in your periphery,

I was waiting for an epiphany and
now I am waiting for death,

the casket doesn't heal me,
I'm taking one more breath,

What releases me, what spells me,
what am I saving for, but
sanctity,

and seriously,
where is the heart
in a poem written
with one eye

March 23, 2017

DECENCY

I awoke to rain!

Oh the heavens they know me! sing for me! Glory!

Oh I'm a snail licking coldly the sidewalk, it is holy,

I'm a girl with short temper, I'm a wick, I'm a fuse,

I was born with one great talent and this talent I shall use,

and the heart is a refuge, and it's really its own land. And when I ask for rain, the planets do the same. I was born on Earth Day, and the heavens know my name, I've been here for so long, but it's somewhere else I lay. And so a kiss to every dragon, there's nothing to be slain. I fall upon this earth,

I'm the princess of the rain.

March 24, 2017

Disreality:

I am like the other fish in that I swim in a sea of an unknown melody, of pain,

Pain pain pain pain pain............

I swim in it like it's the air and for a fortnight I have not breathed.

March 25, 2017

DECENCY

The Incarnation

I think my eyes are changing again,
as they changed from blue, to green, and almost to brown,
now they change to glass, still hot from being weld

I am a kaleidoscope and so every day I take a picture of myself, thinking that perhaps if I collect two thousand of them I will be able to ascertain the sum.

I made a pact with a small green man who lived in the clearing of a forest I only found once: I gave him two pennies and a breakfast cake, and he gave me the eyes of another so I could catch a glimpse of myself.

And then ten years later I sought him again: from my own eyes poured water, I'd forgotten my name. I emptied my pockets and promised a child, he peered into the keyhole in my bosom and told me: Lucrezia, your name is Lucrezia.

On a clear night I was canonized and then I was real: in a veil I surrender to the only ideal. The Catholics murmured "Saint Lucrezia" and I let myself be real.

("I'm here," I whispered. "I'm here I'm here I'm here")

March 25, 2017

www.ingramcontent.com/pod-product-compliance
Lightning Source LLC
LaVergne TN
LVHW011215080426
835508LV00007B/797